THE INTIMATE HORROR OF RELATIONSHIPS

-HAUNTED POEMS FOR THE NOTHING-

(BITTER THOUGHTS ON LOVE AND ALL OF THE SWEET LITTLE LIES)

BY

MIGUEL BIZARRE

© 2009

Note for Librarians: A cataloguing record for this book is available from Library
and Archives Canada at www.collectionscanada.ca/amicus/index-e.html

Printed in Victoria, BC, Canada.

ISBN: 978-1-4251-8633-3

*Our mission is to efficiently provide the world's finest, most comprehensive book publishing
service, enabling every author to experience success. To find out how to publish your book, your
way, and have it available worldwide, visit us online at www.trafford.com*

Trafford rev. 9/25/2009

 www.trafford.com

North America & international
toll-free: 1 888 232 4444 (USA & Canada)
phone: 250 383 6864 ♦ fax: 812 355 4082

ABOUT THE AUTHOR WHO IS AN INCREDIBLE FOOL...

Sort through the fiction and facts that I present. Pick and choose what you desire. Take the truth, take the fiction or a combination of both. Whatever you want to believe and how you choose to view me is your choice. I have no control of whether you know me or not. I am just a vision. Your vision at this moment. Imaginary or not...

I AM:

Fool, Public Property, Slut Monkey, loser, idiot, space cadet, PowerNoise addict,crack baby, BMX rider, music fiend, animal lover,confused,smile addict, lush, Farscape junkie, unemployed, crack dealer-(grape flavored only), pimp, hooker, Swinger,medical worker, volunteer, gay-bi-lesbian-transexual advocate-lover, radical, vegetarian, people lover, movie producer, most inconsiderate person anyone alive can meet, nice to ghosts, co-worker hater, diva, user of emotions, Kathy Griffin and Fairuza Baulk's stalker I'm so Ninja their publicists don't know, homeless advocate, emotional nutcase, anti-Bush (not the one between your legs...lol), late for everything by 1-3 hours, boi toy, homeless, legalize weed supporter, Mt. bike Fool, Reverend, Sober and drunk at the same time (yeah I just might be that talented but you need to hang out with me to see!!!), loner, Seizure survivor, P.E.T.A. advocate, mansion resident, fluid dancer, notorious, hates traveling, promiscuous, shy boy, U.F.O. abductee and survivor damn that probe hurt my rectum couldn't they use lube, Supa-Star, Dolemite's mentor, laid back, former Odyssey Records employee, Black market

Kangaroo penis broker, embraces family values, Double Down Saloon patron, eternally numb, electronica addict, missing Fucky Lausen M.D.(Bucky), missing my friends always, attention whore, just a plain whore as well, princess hater, emotional basket case, wannabe, Gin addict, Mother Tongue's # 3 fan (Shane is # 1), Nidey's future ex-husband, hippie child, flame thrower, soccer player, Mother Nature's bastard step-child, Strip club vet, trendy followers despiser, swears never to drink again, Invader Zim fan, Why do I always end up in this situation idiot, I see dead or imaginary people from time to time (even in pictures), Down for Samoa and all my lil cousins, Boo-Ya Tribe fan, Vegas native, Care about way too many people, go-between, best friend, Angel, grunge lover, Want to be sober for a day, Love New Rocks, Adidas & Vans to death, flying over backyards, world traveler, Howard Stern fan, Mt. climber, pilot, museum curator, lost in thought, kilt/skirt wearing fool, gas guzzler, Ihop diner, P.S.- Did I mention PowerNoise??? and MOTHER TONGUE the best live band ever
more to come...
And finally for now I am Miguel Bizarre nothing worth your time but annoying as Hell like a blister in your groin. (please don't lance me with a rusted needle dipped in rattlesnake venom with Smurf saliva???)

Contact and Haunt me at:
www.myspace.com/miguelbizarre
and/or miguel@miguelbizarre.com

An ExTrA SpEcIaL ThAnKs to:
Denise Jeanne Chaunt Augustine for Editing this mess
and bugging the hell out of me to
finish or attempt to try the next two books...

DEDICATIONS

I would like to thank the following
In no particular order
For touching my life
In some way or another
Life can be so beautiful:
My Dad for being there no matter how much I messed up
R.I.P. I MISS YOU
My Mom for raising me the right way
And loving me
I LOVE YOU SO MUCH
My brother Jerry for EVERYTHING!!!
Myspace.com/jfrobertsphotgraphy
BUCKY FU' AMELEKE LAUSEN!!!
Feb 25, 1976 – May 27, 1998
Wish you were here…
SO MANY OF US MISS YOU!!!
Everyday!!!
You were always my boy…
R.I.P.
Britta for 5 years of Heaven & Hell
Jennifer for showing me true love and belief in a human
and that you can trust someone
through those 8 years we were together
Shawn for all the BS and crazy times
We have been through
Good and bad since you were 13
Trena for being a great friend
TEAM THOMAS:
Rudy
Carrin
Bob(Penny & Ben)

Tony "Beeker" Crocket
(and family)
Kevin Nozar
(this is how I mentally made it)
Bless you brother
-Mother Tongue-
Christian
Davo
Bryan
Sasha
Geoff
For making
The most intense beautiful music
The Peak Show
For the divine music coupled with
Wonderful personalities
Petra Arnold
Holland & Front Row
You two are incredible & talented people
Jilly
LeeAnnarama
For being down to earth & honest people
In this world of so many fakes
Cynthia
For being an incredible human being
With an open mind and a heart of white gold
You are so one of a kind, Best wishes my friend
Dead or Alive (Something in My House...Rip It Up!!!)
Steven
For being the quiet little one
Who got crazy no matter what
(Especially at Suicidal, Infectious, and the Phunk Junkeez)
You had so much to offer the world…
R.I.P.

Roxy my little sister in radiology
Hope you are doing well wherever you are
Inna, Kim and Denise!!!
3 of the best co-workers ever.
(Beautiful souls inside and out)
April C. Sutton
(an incredible friend and writer)
Nidey my punkette future ex-wife
Crystal & Michael
Necie & Lex
(someday we'll roll again lol)
Monica & Lennon
Goddess Amy
Mr. Cellophane
Johnny Pumpkin
Chissum Worthington
Lord Scud & Amanda
DJ Malice
Smokey
Hot Amy
Miss Amy
Dusty and Bryan @ COFFIN IT UP
Rick & Ron Crider & their Awesome Mom
Teo Martinez
Pam the Angry Feminist
(Who so fucking rocks. I adore you!!!)
Jill
Stellar Corpse-Shannon
Kasper-Kelly
Rovilyn
For being a great friend and understanding
My sad pathetic ways
(Even though you are a Princess)
Corina
Abhorrent Existence / DJ Desolous

Mo'
Doug De Nada
Julie-Smoo
Patrick
Jeff Parfitt Hooker # 2
Barnaby-DJ Rust Ryu
Darzon
Matteo
Carmen (gorgeous beyond words inside and out!!!)
DJ Pierrorist (an incredible lad period!!!)
Marisa (one of the most sweetest creations alive)
Caryn Cheesecake
Vincent Adonis
Mr. and Mrs. Moroni
Sarina & DJ Disdain
Maggie
Bronx Bettie
Countess Nessa
Shotgun Shaney
Spizzarri
Luis Allen
Maya
DJ Allen
DJ Morning Star
DJ Razorslave
Rojas
Lucky McMuscles
Colby
Teresa and Tari
Anya
Mina
DJ Liquid Grey aka Lance
Stephanie /@theblckgrl
Pedi

All Hail Bob
Maurice Porter
Ashley (in Texas now miss you friend)
Anabel of the Ball
Shaun Denton
Ida
Joseppe
Pearry Teo Reginald
Yvonne Ortiz
Kai
Matt Beard
Mari and Lu
Felipe Smith (MBQ for Life!!!)
The Charon aka Sharon
and so many more.
I have met so many breath taking people
Thanks for being so kind and wonderful to me
I will and still cherish you all…
The Double Down Saloon
Dino's
The following bands
Whether I personally know them or not.
For making beautiful soul stirring music
That has helped me and I am sure so many others
Enjoy life:
MOTHER TONGUE
sLaYv AxIs
Velvet Acid Christ
:Wumpscut:
Krash Karma
The Mormons
Bang Sugar Bang
STP
BOY HITS CAR

Pu$$y Cow
Danzig
H.I.M.
My Ruin
The Peccadilloes
Monster Magnet
Howard Jones
Silver Needle
Aslan Faction
Psyclone_9
Combichrist
Terrorfakt
Sisters of Mercy
Skinny Puppy
Y-Luk-O
Otherwise
The Reverend Rob Ruckus
Shooter Jennings
(and all outlaws of country)
Mark Hornsby the coolest promoter
and so many more
Suicidal Tendencies
RHCP
Public Enemy
BDP
Just-Ice
King Sun D. Moet
Too Short
Schoolly D.
Eric B. & Rakim
AC/DC
Def Poetry Jam

Bratster for being you
You are my light in life
All of the poets & writers of the world
Who share their thoughts on Paper
Voice and Soul
The Black Widows of Vegas
Jenny-O
Nidey
Shanda
Christina
Nikki
Sarah
A few amazing authors I don't know personally
but inspired me beyond belief.
The first two made me want to write again.
Their writing and talent is so amazing.
Hart D. Fisher
Christa Faust
Roberta Lannes
(She so rocks!!!)
Lucy Taylor
Poppy Z. Brite
Jhonen Vasquez
Charlee Jacob
Lance Carbuncle
And of course:
Clive Barker

And to my fake "Heaven"
Without you showing your true self
I would never have known this hell
What goes around comes around;
KARMA
Hope you feel 1/10th of the pain you caused me

THE INTIMATE HORRORS OF RELATIONSHIPS:

BEAUTIFUL SADNESS
CAPTURED EMOTIONS
HOOKS
VALUE INSIDE
JUST ONE WISH
SCRATCH
GHOSTS
TO REPLACE
PHOTOGRAPH
LOST CAUSE IN AN EMPTY ROOM
PEDESTAL
AN ANGEL
LOST YOU THERE
WAS IT WORTH IT
ANNOYED
PASSION
A STEP
HOW DEEP IS THIS???
WHERE DID I GO
EXORCISE MY DEMONS
BOTTLE
HEART
ADDICTED
YOUR EVIL WAYS
ALL I WANTED
DREAMING OF YOU
FAKE CALLS
WEEKEND IS HERE

DAYBREAK
WISH
A DARK PLACE
FLESH 1.0
CLEANSED
SLEEP TIGHT
CONTACT ME
TIRED
FRIEND
WHAT BULL SHIT
CAN (CAN'T SEEM TO FIND)
DEATH
INTENSITY
FULL CIRCLE
HOLD ME
TURN
AT THIS TIME
EARLY MORNING
TORTURED
BETTER
DO YOU?
USER
EVERYBODY HAS SOMEBODY
IN TEARS
FIRE
HALLOWEEN
AUG 8th
FREEDOM CELL
FUTURE
PICTURES OF YOU
DECEIT
SIX FEET UNDER
FUCKING FUCKER

FARSCAPE
TO THE ONE THAT MATTERS
SIMPLE
FUCKED IN MY MIND
ROUTINE
HAPPY
NO CHANGES
OPEN SHUTTERS
REMINDED
HATE
MUSIC IS MY SAVIOR
I'M SCARED
SAD
SELFISH
IT GETS BORING
OTEP
KEEP YOU BUSY
TO REPLACE
THE CONSEQUENCE
SOMEHOW MUSIC
SHOW
TASTE
THE DAY AFTER
TO BE KNOWN
TAKEN AWAY
THE 13th
SKINDRED
SEE
STANDING TO THE SIDE

BEAUTIFUL SADNESS

Would I feel this way if I never?

Never what you ask?

Never met you

Never felt you tap my shoulder

Never heard you ask what cologne I was wearing

Never stood at that side of the stage

Never exchanged numbers

Never bothered to call you

Never become enchanted by your beauty

When I saw you again 3 months later

Where would I be?

Who would I be with?

Would I be happier?

Would I never feel this pain?

Would I have shed these tears

Full of honesty and pure love

Would my soul be this black?

Would my heart be slowly decaying?

Crumbling away…

Rotting…

Cracking…

Falling to pieces…

Would my despair be this intense?

Would my love have been this intense?

From the most incredible high to the

Worst low any being can feel

The worst that I have ever known

A surreal exploration in life.

Would I have agreed that it was worth it?

Would I pound the ground with hate?

Asking why must I feel this!?!?!?

What is it to be so into another soul?

You'll never know

I've felt it all…despite your betrayal

I have tasted both

I guess I am in a beautiful sadness

CAPTURED EMOTIONS

An expensive high

That's all you really were

But an addict doesn't know they are addicted

Doesn't know the pain that they are causing to their self

They just want that pleasure

Just for one more final time

Make me feel good again

Make me love to be alive

So over & over again I am your slave

Slave to your illusionary love

Depressed and low when you are not around

So buzzed & happy when I see you

Let me have one more hit

Inject your false love into my soul for the last time

Don't leave me in ruin

Twisting and groaning in pain

Wanting what I can't have

Hoping for a savior to ease this torment

Come & take a look at the other side

If your fear doesn't stop you

Total erasure is what I seek

Of all the memories that I own of you

I've committed nothing against you

So why do you steal them from me

Robbed me of my emotions and left me on my back

In the middle of the street and I can't be saved

My freedom no longer exists

What to do?

End this now

Show me some mercy

Please pay one of your little fuck friends

So they can shoot me in the head

And put a stop to this roller coaster

That only heads in one final direction

The deepest level of Hell

HOOKS

What do you do when you are wrapped

Wrapped around their little finger

Everything about them is what you want

Everything about them is what you desire

They are all you can see

You just flow with it

Deal with whatever comes your way

Like an insect trapped in a glass jar

You can see it all but there is no way out

Like a hemorrage in your brain you didn't know was there

But eventually the effects increase

And you feel the pain

You never hear it

But when lightning strikes

It sets every nerve on fire

You tingle all over

The venomous tingle of hurt & betrayal

Standing alone on a desolate highway

The semi comes out of nowhere and strikes on target

Six lanes and you happen to be in the wrong one

Lying on the ground as it speeds away

Never to be seen

So close your eyes and wish them away

Hope they never enter your life again

They don't deserve to know you

Unless you want to feel more pain

Once you rip away from the hooks embedded in you

Don't look back to see how much flesh…

How much flesh you've left behind

Because if you do

They always win…

Just walk away

They don't deserve to know you

You are much more precious than that

That perfect dark angel is out there

You just met the wrong one

VALUE INSIDE

What is it that we each have

Swirling around in your thoughts, blood, heart and mind

Deep inside our physical creation

That isn't physical or material

Yet you know it exists in us all

Spiritual maybe?

Mental maybe?

Yet another human can touch a person

Like nothing else....

Good or bad you know it when you feel it

Ghostly, heavenly, wicked, cursed, enchanting

Which do you feel now?

It makes you so aware of everything

Or maybe it's so good you just sit and wonder

Just enjoying the ecstasy when it is there

Hoping it will never end

Or wishing it would cease to exist

Blessed with pleasure unknown

Or

Haunted with distraught emotions

It can rearrange every single thought

Redirect your route in life

Push or pull you closer or farther to them

Put them on a pedestal or in the gutter

Bring tears of joy or tears of pain

Send a chill across your body when they bat their eyes

Or strangle your aura with an evil grin

Comfort your sleep with thoughts swirling in your skull

Or make you thrash left & right on your bed

All night long refusing the Sandman's duty

Positive or negative

Everyone has that value inside

My own has been ruined beyond repair

By what you have deep in your burning black crevices

I don't want to know it anymore

Let me be free again

JUST ONE WISH

That's all I ask for

That's all I need

That's what I want

That's all that would make it better

For me

Or maybe someone else

But what should I ask for?

For world peace?

That no one ever is born disabled

That only the bad worthless people die

Die a violent death for the suffering they have caused others

That no one has to starve in life

That no one has to experience poverty

That no one has to see

See your parents suffer through

Through deteriorating health, disease and die

That every single parent alive never has to lose and see their child

go to the embracing arms of death

That depression never existed

That there are no homeless

That no one experiences a violent death

That there was no racism

That all wars came to a halt

That those that died for this country came back to life

So their families wouldn't suffer the loss of life they have

experienced

That super stores never existed

That there was no top 40 pop bullshit

That 90% of America would stop being so damn judgmental

That there were no asshole people in the world

Well I guess it's my turn to be selfish

Above all that I mentioned I do truly wish for from the bottom of

my

Heart

Although all I wish for right now…

Is that you call me

And apologize for what you have done

SCRATCH

On my mind

You are always wandering there

Looking deep down trying to find a crack

So you can bury yourself deep inside

Lodging your memories in me so they don't die

Keep me on, hook, line and sinker

A zombie that doesn't know right from wrong

Lost & bewildered still looking for the one

So here I am still thinking you are it

Your brainwashing has rinsed my thoughts clean

Whatever was left of any others is totally gone

You and your evil ways know what to do

Insuring yourself there is no competition

A smile on your face because you think you know how to play the

game

Lies, sex, betrayal, deceit and false hopes

Don't talk to me of the future when it doesn't exist

You're so messed up as a human being

You breathe and live yet you are not real

An illusion to keep me around

A joke that I wasn't aware of

A gift from the foulest place

A trap to destroy all that is good

A barrel of lies

A snake in the grass to charm me with its deciet

The devil's personal play thing

You know what you are

And for the time being

You are an itch

An itch I can't scratch

But if I ever could

I'll rub my skin raw

Til I bleed

Until you are finally gone

GHOSTS

I sit here with tears running down my face

Not really sad yet not really happy

I sit here and see images

Images of you walking by

Images of you laying on my bed

Images of you eating food

As we sit before the TV

Images of you at the bar ordering our drinks

Images of you next to me at the front of the stage

Images of you next to me in the movie theatre

Images of you parking your car outside

Images of you walking to my door

Images of you with your arms open wide

A smile on your face, maybe happy to see me

Images of you looking deep into my eyes

With that false love that I thought was true

But it didn't matter it felt real at the moment

Images of you at the concert talking to everyone

Being your free spirited self

I adored you and your ways

Images of you leaving in the morning to work

Images of you sleeping so deeply

Images of you with your head resting on my chest

Images of your body so delicate & wonderful

Laying next to me at 3:00AM

What more could I ask for??

I was so happy & content

Now I am in a chaotic disaster

Not just "Haunted when the minutes drag"

I'm haunted all the time

Things that will never be real

Ghosts of your presence

Nothing I can do but miss you

Can I die quietly now…???

TO REPLACE

Why do I need this?

Why is it the only thing?

I need someone there...

Someone everyday

Someone to call me for no reason

Call me just to say hi!!!

Someone I think about as soon as I awake

Someone I'm thinking of as I fall asleep

Someone who crosses my mind

More than the natural male's thoughts of sex

Someone who I will truly miss

Even though it's only an hour that has gone by

Someone who I can trust

Someone who I know cares

Someone who will hug me tightly

Someone who actually wants me to be happy

Someone who wants to share their life

Someone who knows what they want

Someone who won't turn their back on me

Someone who I know will be there

Someone who will make me forget about "you"

Someone to erase you from my mind

It's been a year

And I haven't found them yet

I'm so fucked…..THANKS!!!

PHOTOGRAPH

What does it hold?

Something of significance?

A photograph captured an image of us

Somewhere, someplace, sometime

No longer that memory resides

Resides in your mind

You have already buried it with new ones

From new people that you continue to meet

In your tiny little mind

The one that never has regret

Fading like corrosion into the past

So many little things in the picture

All of them bring back a different memory

A flashback to a time of excitement

A serene moment in time

A night so dark and surreal

The studded wristband I gave you

The clothes I dressed you in

Jewelry that lost its sparkle

The fishnet clinging close to you

The drink in your tiny little hand

The smile on your face

All of it adds up to something once beautiful

How can a picture capture, hold, & contain?

Contain the happiness for eternity

So that anyone alive can see it even years from now

Can that actually happen between two people

Where the memories shared

Are more than enough

Than a piece of paper with an image on it

Locked in an immortal safe of beauty

Or is it an illusion

I want that

Can someone?

Somehow unlock it please...

LOST CAUSE IN AN EMPTY ROOM

A drink in my hand another time

Exactly the same as yesterday but a different moment

My mind wanders all over again

Thoughts that I don't really need up in there

Wondering again about my choices in life

Why did I make them

Can I rearrange?

Should I even talk to you at all

After all the things you have put me through

Why should I allow you to invade my space?

You've called 3 times but I choose to refuse

Refuse to call you and fall in your trap

Just go away and leave me alone

Step away from my world and stay in yours

Play with your fake pretty club people

And those bouncers you just love to death

Have fun at their expense and stop tempting me

Cut the chain you have attached to my heart

It needs to rust in peace all alone

My sanity has escaped me so long ago

Running away on and on

I was nothing before

So what's different now?

You can't explain that

The future is now and you don't belong here

You'll always be the same uncaring individual

Just looking out for yourself

Not worried about karma

But you will some day

What goes around comes around

It will hit you like a brick

Flying at 90mph

Right into your face of deceit

As you fall over

You will become the lost cause

No one cares about

PEDASTAL

You want to be on a throne

So every idiot will worship you

Kiss your punk ass

Give you all the attention and more

So you'll know about everything

...and miss nothing

Is it that pathetic

That you have to be in everyone else's business

You can't miss one damn thing in life

Because it all centers around you

And only you

The Queen of Nothing

Your servants the losers in life

Like myself, the biggest loser to exist

You want to be the one that's loved by all

But that will never happen when you can't

Can't love your family and friends who are real

The ones that actually did care about you

At one time in your little fantasy world

People are remembered for the things they have done

And sorry to break it to you

YOU HAVEN'T DONE SHIT

For one single person dead or alive

Oh wait…Yes you have

You've done it all for yourself

Too bad that doesn't mean anything to anyone

Except those super wonderful

I can do anything for you, I'll be there no matter what, I love all

of you Til you fuck them

Which is usually the same night

Or 3 days at the most

So if in reality you are the true loser

With no goal or direction in life

Then why I am unhappy???

FUCK YOU!!!

AN ANGEL

Once in the past you said I was an Angel

I saw it in your eyes

You actually meant something you said

For once…how things change

Sent to be there for you no matter what

You adored everything about me

You couldn't believe I was real

We had so much fun

You asked me to be yours

Life was good

We had nothing to complain about

I fell in love with you

You meant everything to me

We shared so many times that were unreal

Surreal moments that will never be duplicated

I trusted with no lingering doubts

What more could I ask for

Then somehow, somewhere, sometime

This angel fell from your grace

I didn't do anything wrong

It was something you just had to do

You stood there smiling

Then when I turned around

With my confidence lowered

My guard was down

You put the knife in my back

Pushing it through my heart

Tears of blood & love

Poured from my eyes

Wondering....

Why? Why? Why?

You stayed silent because you had no answer

I guess my wings were tarnished

I was no longer that pure thing you saw in your deceitful eyes

You got bored with this Angel...

May I finally die now...please?

LOST YOU THERE

The happiness in my heart

It was so overwhelming

Every centimeter of my fiber was alive

Alive with thoughts of you

You could see it in my eyes & smile

Sometimes it scared you

Knowing that someone was so in love with you

You were my all & everything

I adored you so much with all of my dark minded soul

Anything in the world

I would have done for you

Even now perhaps I still would have

In many ways I did so much

From the very beginning

When you locked your keys in your car

On that hot day

At the hospital

I took care of the situation

All those times you were so drunk

At 3:30AM your friends call

And I was there to pick you up from the club

Just wanted to make sure you were safe

Just wanted to make sure you were happy

Just wanted to make sure you were comfortable in life

All I wanted was the best for you

Give you some kind of security in a friend you can trust

I wasn't asking for much at all

If there was honesty

Things would have been different

We would still be friends at least

Guess somewhere along the way

I lost you there

With someone new in your life

I wasn't anything special

And never will be

WAS IT WORTH IT?

Over and over

You tell me things that give me hope

That you have something good inside you

That you may actually have the capacity to care

But just like life & death

The only thing that can be really guaranteed in life...

It dies!!!

Dies away never to be seen

You never have made up for one thing

My birthday alone in L.A.

Had the nerve to call me

Didn't even remember it was my B-day

As usual there is something or someone

That's more important

Every single time

That's the only thing I know for sure about you

Your mind wanders to whoever is before you

It doesn't matter for how long you have known them

I'm not good enough to be your lover

I'm not good enough to be your best friend

Yet once in the past I was both

Now I am not and you can't explain why

…..but I think this is it

6/20/2004 you didn't show or call in time

I visited the grave without you

Someone's there buried in the Earth

That someone actually showed you respect

Yet the day after he passed away til now

You haven't shown one ounce of it towards him

I guess you are that shallow and calloused

Remember that you promised to visit with me

Was your weekend adventure worth it?

Add one more thing you never made up

I guess that's why we weren't meant to be

I have a soul

You never did

Good-bye for eternity

You lost someone who was devoted to you….

ANNOYED

Thinking about the past

All the things you've done

And still you're not regretting

Not a fucking single one

It never really mattered to you

Just something for you to do

Nothing else around

Nothing else to experience

I was just a novelty

A toy to keep you amused

Yet like a stupid fool

I kept you in my life

Hoping maybe someday

You'll see the wrong that you have done

Tell me something that you would never say

Well that will never happen

Your nightlife is too precious

Too sacred for you to give up

All of the perks you treasure

The pleasure between your thighs

Of someone new and different

Which in the end I could have dealt with

But I was never number one

More like # 17

I wanted something concrete

Until now

You're gone, no longer present

But do you really care??

Hell no!!!

I'm a fading thought

Smoke disappearing magically

In front of your eyes

Never to be seen again

And you'll never think of me

As you move on to the person across the room

Your eyes locked upon them…

PASSION

It's inside of me boiling over

Passion for life

Passion for music

Passion of loving all those around me

Passion for writing

Passion for the dead

Passion to express myself

Passion for creating

Passion to make a stranger smile

Passion fueled by your scorn

Passion that fuels my fire

The emotions erupt in me constantly

Like a volcano unpredictable

Any time, Any hour, Any place

It flows like an untamed river

Searching for that beach

The one that is the paradise

Hoping and hoping to land on its sands

It just flows and flows

On and on

I'll never find it

But I will keep trying

For the life of me and more

I need and want it

In the mean time I'll make do

Somehow someway I'll channel this

Channel it to a positive vibe

You'll see me again

And I hope you regret…

(That's a huge monster sized hope that I ask for)

Regret taking me for granted

But you won't and never will

It's not your style

Because you have nothing in your heart for yourself

Or anyone else…

A STEP

Well this is it

The weekend I step away

Spend it with someone new

Far from this city

Far from your reach

You won't exist for awhile

Or so I hope

Maybe we'll connect

Have so much fun together

Well….actually I have

We've hung out before

After you fucked me over

But you were still on my mind

Haunting the deepest recesses

Taunting me with your vile cruelty

So I wasn't totally there

After the night together

Now I will give 100% of me

They deserve it

But do I deserve them?

We all know it's true

No matter what or who

There's always someone better

You've found that out

Around 5 to 10 times

Oh wait

Well it's my turn

To be in the company of someone

Who acts their age

And appreciates things

That isn't a follower

With no direction in life

Poor, broke, and lonely

I hope that becomes you

Good luck you fucking user

HOW DEEP IS THIS???

You wonder how deep is my love

You've seen it in my eyes

Glossy & glazed like I was high on something

Your synthetic love that never really existed

That's what fueled my addiction

My love was so deep

That you could go into the deepest ocean

And no matter how hard you looked

You would never find the bottom

So deep that you couldn't find an explanation

Even if you memorized the Webster's dictionary

You would still be lost

In the shuffle of meaningless definitions

That will never mean anything to you

So deep that on a moon lit night

You could stare at the most distant star

And see and know that my love…

It travels on so far past it

So deep you could witness a 3 car collision

In slow motion as their lives come to an end

And still not know what the emotions feel like

My love glows more brightly than their souls floating away

Off into heaven because they are truly the only innocent ones

Looking and searching for a place to rest

So deep that I open every door for you

So deep that if your car breaks down

I am there

So deep that if you lose your job

I'll take care of you

So deep that nothing seems impossible

My love is so deep

Beyond what you could ever comprehend

And you are so shallow

You'll never really see it

Ever....

Your soul is quicksand full of decaying bodies

WHERE DID I GO...

Once I was alive, healthy happy, strong

An outgoing being

Enjoyed all that the night & day had to offer

Now it's a facade

Sublime feelings and thoughts

Tucked away for only myself to know

Even the few I trusted

Knew nothing at all

I have kept it hidden so well

No one really knows

Not even you

The one that I thought was real

But I know that you don't care

You have places to go

People to see and be seen with

And you were my other half

Now you are gone

Drifted apart and away

Nowhere to be seen

When I clock out and head home

And make that lonely drive

Music playing as it always will

Pondering over the past

Trying to relive what was good

Wondering what went wrong

Then accepting that it will never be again

It has dissolved into time

Faded away for eternity

The sad returns

Knowing you won't be calling

As you did everyday

Knowing you won't be there

To meet me ever again.

In the mirror

That being no longer exists….

He is so dead…

UNTIL IT'S GONE

I'm there for you

No matter what

You know that so damn well

You take it all for granted

Knowing I will be at your feet with a snap of your fingers

When you have a problem

I'll try my hardest to solve it

I'll do my all to make things right

When you have nothing else to do

You know I'll be there to occupy your time

No matter where or what I am doing

You look in the mirror and see flaws

Yet when I look at you

Even with painful tortured eyes

Tears of blood invisible to you

I see nothing but perfection in heaven

Words from my lips have never put you down

Physically and mentally I adore you for you

Through all the pain and the torture

Of the emotional hurricane you create

I still stand trying to prove myself

Hoping one day you will see I am the one

I am real and I will do all I can in life

To make you happy

But how can I make you happy if I am not

It's the sad result of fate and reality

It's something I must accept

You will never change or see through crystal clear eyes

Your ways are clouded and will always be

The storm of your life will never cease

Yet I try to hang on as my emotions bleed

But it's a losing battle

My love is like blood, it doesn't last forever

Dripping from my veins until it's gone…

EXORCISE MY DEMONS

Why am I doing this?

Why do I write?

What good does it do?

Will anyone ever read this and understand

Know the pain that I have felt

Look into the dark sky and say

"I have been there I know the feeling."

Most likely not

These are my secret burdens

No one else needs to deal with this shit

Who else really cares

No they don't at all

So why do I do this?

Maybe I need to…

Maybe I have to…

For this past relationship that has savaged my heart and mind

That exploded like a napalm bomb

Coating me with its sickness

It's so far past beyond and over

But the effects are still there

Burning, festering, hurting, and taunting

Letting me know I was the fool

I was the idiot who believed

That there are true good things in life

Hoping that true romance does exist

But I am an unremarkable knight in dull dented armor

My head hung down in shame

I know where I stand

I stand with it…

Loneliness is a demon

An evil one who wants its reward

And this time it's me

Wrapped around me

Flowing through my veins

It's enjoying life

While I suffer

BOTTLE

Two empty bottles I throw away

Every 24 hours

Like an alcohol-fueled clock

That needs to be refilled

So it can run in stealth mode

Cover my sorrows

In a sea of liquid fire

That burns my eyes

And it doesn't make me forget

It makes me remember more

Everything amplified

Beyond what I can handle

So I keep drinking

Until I feel good again

Until I open 2 more bottles

Tomorrow to start all over

The nightmare begins again

Tormenting with visions that I do not desire

The truth and how you really were

The games you played

The lies you have told

Repeatedly saying that you would prove yourself

Somehow you would earn my trust again

Yet it never happened

You destroyed it even more

Continued with more lies

So I grab another flask

Put it to my mouth

Hoping for the moment

That temporary amnesia takes me over

Where I feel good for a moment in time

Where nothing can hurt me again

Where the cemetery of lies and deceit no longer exist

The liquor fog is thick

Nowhere in my vision

Nowhere to be seen

You are no longer there

HEART

The stadium of my heart was always there

So vast and huge always there for you

Beating in rhythm to your every breath

Unity so full of love

You could walk into it and not worry

Worry about the hate in the world

Not worry about anyone else being there

It's red blooded passion flowed for you

It was for you and only you

The love poured on and on

Your own fountain of tranquility

Pure crystal clear emotions

That reached the highest level of joy in the human soul

More life than drops of blood from an angel

Dedicated to you and you

Over and over again

Standing there proud and confident

My emotions were all 100% yours

Locked up

Your own tomb of love

Nothing could have taken that commitment away

No matter where or what I was doing

You knew you were on my mind

You were always near in thought

You were the one that I missed

You were the one that I desired

You were the one that I needed

You were the one that I wished was there with me

My heart was like a black velvet blanket to wrap around you

Keep you warm from the cold of the world

Keep you smiling with my honesty

Keep you secure from deceit

Keep you safe from all that is wrong

I just wish I knew the truth

Knew that it was you…

You were the wrong

ADDICTED

7:10PM and I wonder why

That you might not call

I already know you won't

We are done forever

Even as acquaintances

Never to be friends again

Listening to V.A.C.

Trying to leave this place behind

Deep inside my mind

I know it will be so hard

Yet I can't let it all go

But I know I need to

Stop this sickness

Stop the addiction

I don't want to be addicted to you

You are a bad habit that has poisoned every nerve

Blinded my eyes

So that all I see is you

You know what you are doing

You know my emotions are on a death bed

Yet you won't let me go

When it accommodates you

You then decide to call

Used to be 4 to 5 days a week

Then 2 days a week

Then once every 2 weeks

Now it's once a month

Just let it go

I'm not your type of person

You have

Better things to do

Better people to see

Better places to go

Do something once in your life

For someone other than yourself

Leave me alone…

YOUR EVIL WAYS

Your so called love-

A bodily sensation that causes:

Acute discomfort or suffering

You make me feel pain

You make my mind blurry

You make me hurt inside

You make my heart crack & crumble

You make me sad

You make the tears carry the blood away from my heart

That is already dying away

You make me weak

You make me sleepy from the misery

You make a grave look inviting

You make me confused

You make anyone look like a saint next to you

You make me wonder why

You make me lose all hope with life

You make me insecure

You make me feel ugly

You make me feel worthless

You make me feel hideous inside and out

You make me miserable

You make me depressed

You make me feel low

You make me anxious

You make me feel unknown

You make me feel broken

You make me feel battered

You make me hate all that is good

You make me angry with rage

Because you never hear a word I say

You make me dread the next night

Because you won't be there

Yet you say you care

I guess it's just your evil ways

ALL I WANTED

Just one person to trust

Someone to share everything with

Accept my love deep in their heart

Embrace me as a lover and a friend

Look forward to seeing me everyday

Actually believe there is true love

Deep within share their thoughts

Tragedy or pleasure

Willing to share

Share what's on their minds

Not ashamed to speak the truth

Someone who thinks about me

Someone who needs me

Someone who wants me

Someone to travel the world with

Someone I can be around

And they actually want me there

Someone to sit at home and watch a video

Or maybe out to see a concert

Or play pool at the Double Down

Travel cross-country

Visiting haunted places

Houses, cemeteries, towns

New Orleans, New York, L.A., S.F.

But you couldn't even try

Just a lazy pathetic person

Physically, mentally & emotionally

Too much work for you to deal with

So many other things & people on your mind

I'll always be a waste of time in your eyes

But somewhere

Out there

I know there is someone better

I'm just waiting to meet them

But I probably never will

I'm too lost to know when it does happen…

DREAMING OF YOU

The blanket of black

Takes over my mind

I drift off into the dark

Then somewhere somehow

We're together

Recreating scenes from the past

Times I thought

We both enjoyed

Times I thought were real

The laughter and smiles

Then it's 4:00AM

I wake up in the pitch black

Turn on the purple lights

You're not next to me

I was only dreaming of you…

My subconscious mind

Working in ways I can not control

Ways in which I wish I could put a stop

Nail it down with rusted spikes

Deep in the most far region of my mind

Pour acid over those memories

Let them blister and boil into remnants

That no longer holds any value or appeal

Then perhaps the cold dry winds in my soul will begin

Lashing out and blowing those remains away

Someplace where they belong

A place that they can never be recovered

By myself or anyone else

Let them rot and vanish

They are no use to me

As I was of no use to you

In your life of deceit

So what is the use of this

Why did I bother to store those memories

No idea

Just stupidity and blindness

FAKE CALLS

So you called me today

After you came home

From wherever you spent the night

Doing what you do best

And then worked all day

Then you thought about the night before

You ran into mutual friends last night

Who told you I was there

But you already knew that!!!

You looked right at me

I waved like the dumb idiot

Just being polite

Although on your message

You claimed you didn't

Sincere sounding is what you were

The person I knew a year ago

Almost believed you might care

Almost called you

Despite everything

I still miss you

What would that accomplish???

Nothing for nothing

I know you will never change

Plus you wouldn't be home anyways

So why on your time

You have better to do

A never ending party

So don't pretend to care

You never fucking did!!!

You never will

You never can

You never could

Enjoy your shallow life

Kiss your ghost's good-bye

So they would leave me alone

And let my mind rest in peace

WEEKEND IS HERE

Once again that time has arrived

The weekend those 2 ½ days

You work your ass off all week

So you can enjoy it all

Those so special days

You so treasure more than life

Where nothing else matters at all

It all revolves around your little head

Nothing is more important

It's your ultimate high

More than your own family

Your own life and blood

The time when night is your friend

As it wraps it's arms around you

Squeezing you tight

Making you feel so good inside

That warm feeling tingles all over your body

Guiding to places where it happens

Shake and groove that body

The night life the only thing you know

All the drinks you can consume

All the lips you can kiss

And it still introduces you to more people every time

Every night every hour

Those few days that you do it all

Grinding against whomever comes your way

And your friend…the night

Is there with you as you drive their way

It guides you to their house

As you kiss and grope

Excited by the anticipation

Meeting another new stranger

Now you are ready

For fucking another new experience

We use to share the weekends together

…I HATE THE WEEKEND NOW!!!

DAYBREAK

It's so crazy the sun rises again

The rays shooting right through straight into my room

Like those signature Adidas stripes it will never fade

Over & over it repeats itself

So why do I turn?

Turn over and hope you are there?

Looking for the imprint that your body leaves on the sheets

The light blinds me in my thoughts

Colors in my head spinning & spinning around

I try to swim through them to find you

Hoping I can reach out & grasp your hand

So this madness can stop

Stop the tormenting of my soul

Put a calm to the chaos that creeps through my veins

Even though my heart now is frozen & cold

It can't freeze the pain that radiates from my mind

The ceiling absorbs it & spreads it to the walls

And if these walls could talk

They would recall all the good times that have past

But it's too late to listen

The infection has spread

Spread all over to silence the good that is barely alive

This room is cursed until I burn it down

Or a Goddess of Sin blesses it

The day makes me arise to deal with reality

Hoping once again for something I can never have

To be happy with life again

To be happy with you

No, I give up…

Just let me be happy all alone by myself

And never recall who or what you were to me

You don't deserve to be remembered

With me or anyone alive

Fade away into the sea

Behind the sphere of light

As the sun proceeds to fuck the ocean

WISH

Wish you would hurt

Wish you would become an amputee

Wish your implants would rupture

Wish your life would become more complicated

More than it was already

Wish your face would melt away

Wish your tongue would be cut off

Wish you would cry

Wish you would catch an STD

Wish you would get arrested for

a D.U.I.

Wish your car would fall apart

Wish they would catch your felony conviction

Wish you would lose all your friends

Wish you would lose your pride

Wish you would lose what intelligence you ever had

Wish you would be caught stealing from your work like you

always do

Wish you would become ugly

Wish no one ever looked your way

Wish you were never born

Wish you never moved here

Wished you never knew my friends

Wished you never used me

Wish you would have no money

Wish you would lose your job

Wish you would feel heartbreak

Wish you would actually have a fucking heart

Wish you would feel pain

Wish you would lose your mind

Wish you would understand

Wish you could open your eyes and really see

Wish you would actually acknowledge me

Wish you would let me know you know I am alive

What I really wish is that you would care about me

…That's all I really want

A DARK PLACE

The last 3 days have been a blur

Going so low that I couldn't go

Any further below

From what you have immersed me in

What you have created

For your own pleasure

My own personal hell

Done things so bad

Trying to numb the pain

I want to escape

From this reality

Put the gun to my head

And erase it all

3 days have passed

Haven't heard your voice

Most likely never will

My mind is a little more clear

Gave my brother the gun

Trying to crawl out of

That dark place

Trying to be stable again

Time will tell but it will never

Heal the wounds

The ones you over and over

Inflicted on my dying soul

Through any means possible

I will pollute myself

Liquify my mind

Put myself in a trance

A hazey daze that I can't see out of

So I can never see the truth

Never know the result

Never know the facts

Never know the truth…

That you never did care for me…

FLESH 1.0

Tempt me, seduce me, use me

Why do you do that?

Why am I your target to inflict your tricks?

I don't want you near me at all

And you know that

Yet you call and leave a polite message

Make me think you have changed your ways

Pretend that you are genuine

Act like you miss me so damn much

That I am something special in your life

That you will always need me in some way

So I debate and debate over and over again

Should I call you

Or should I ignore

What am I to do

Why do I have to even deal with this

Why does life wish to fuck with me?!?!?!

I know what the right thing is…

To never acknowledge your attempt to contact me

Pretend that you've never called

Just erase the message that you left

Vanquish your whole existence

Block your number from my phone

So many people that deserve my attention

Just as friends

They would appreciate me for who I am

Unlike you they won't take me for granted

Yet here you are next to me

My arms wrapped around you...

Pretending this isn't a nightmare

In an embrace of confused love

Our hearts entwined in a wicked mist

I wish it would never end

But it will

Because it will never be real

CLEANSED

A Saturday night

I was out & about to see some bands

My little sis was there with her love

One of the bands there was one you know as well

I thought you might show

But no

You and I saw them two years ago

Their very first show

It's so sad that you are not here

But I know it is for the best

There's no point for someone to care for another

When that other only cares about themselves

Saw lots of people we know

It was good to see them

The show started then two hours later

The band Cell played

It was such a moving experience

Even though you weren't next to me

To share it...

Have I been cleansed?

Maybe tonight…

In the night my emotions move on

And separate themselves from what is not real

Moving further into a positive path

Trying to feel life again

Let its wonderful arms wrap around me

Soothe my pain and ease my sorrow

Something you could never accomplish

Something you would never try for anyone

Heartless you may be Death's sister

So cruel and cunning

Obtaining only what you need

Then discarding the carcass of the heart to the side

So that it may decay without love

That's all you know

You never truly knew me…..

SLEEP TIGHT

Suppose to be at a show

One that I was looking forward to be at

But I am not there

I am here

Writing away

Creating the chaotic misery that I know to well

Bullshitting at home

Having a drink

My usual routine

And another drink

Drown the sorrows

Watching the shows

The shows we use to watch together

Laying side by side on the bed

A smile sneaks across my face

Remembering good times we once had

Then it fades away

My eyes shift upwards wondering

And I sit here looking at my clock

It's 11:29PM

You have to work early

But are you even home???

Most likely not

Why should it matter

I am non existent in your eyes

I've been replaced

Emotionally

Then both physically and mentally

I don't exist in your thoughts

You have no regrets

And that hurts me the most

That you hurt me with an intense pain

And you can't even say you are sorry

I hope you sleep tight…

CONTACT ME

So when will you contact me

When will you ever actually miss me

It's been a few weeks

Nothing at all

Few months now

Still nothing

And more nothing from you

The chemistry has been neutralized

No longer the spark in your little evil eyes

Or the visits to the flesh menagerie

Ceased to exist your lust for me

Love has met its death in your cold shallow heart

Yours truly is now alone

You said it would be hard

To stay away from me

But like I said…..

90% of the time you don't think about me

So what's 10% more

You shed those fake crocodile tears

Like you were going to actually miss me

But here I am now

A proven fact that you never had sympathy

Your mission is for your own good

So now I am invisible

Totally forgotten

Real love is not for you

It's something you'll never grasp the nature of

And to think I wasted the duration of two years

On a worthless event

You've got new rich little bitches

Trendy bitch ass friends

So high and mighty

To fuck you all night long

Have fun you fucking traitor

Once upon a time I thought

We were best of friends

TIRED & CONFUSED

So tired of this all

The emotions like a roller coaster

One moment you are all into me

The other moment I don't even exist

You call me and want to spend time together

Then for days you don't bother to call at all

Gone for a weekend then you magically appear

You tell me you miss me

Kiss me on the cheek then lips

But we both know that's not true

It's just words you know I want to hear

From a mouth more potent than cancer

True lies from the deep of your black heart

Carefully manufactured to cover the truth

You've played the game and you play it well

Submerged deep in your hell

My tears just dry up instantly

I can't escape

Your smiling face is all that I see

Looking up I can see you are the perfect thief

The thief of hearts

And you have collected mine

Locked away someplace

That I can never find

Slowly losing it all

What's wrong from right

Confusion and madness on top of the rest

The rest of the feelings causing chaos in my mind

I'm so fucking confused

I'm so fucking tired

Please just leave me alone

Just let me sleep

And then finally wake up from this nightmare

Escape your cruel reality

Hopefully for the last time

FRIEND

Hmmm.........

A friend is someone who cares

Someone who actually worries about their friend

Wonders where they are and what they are doing

Someone who wants to hang out and do things

Someone who tries to make sure they are there for their friend

Someone who shares anything & everything

Someone who wants their friend to know

Someone who knows when their friend is depressed

Someone who doesn't assume their friend will always pay

Someone who appreciates those around them

Someone who appreciates life

And all the beautiful things it offers

Someone who doesn't take people for granted

Someone who doesn't assume shit

Someone who doesn't put partying before their friends

Someone who just cares about their friends

Someone who doesn't put a random fuck ahead of them

Someone with some type of emotion

Someone that's fucking real

Someone that will never be you

Someone that will never be you

Someone that will never be you

And Guess fucking what

You proved yourself to everyone

You aren't shit and never will be

You use and lose in the end

Take what you can and kiss it away

I have learned so much

In the lessons that life taught me concerning you

Here you go:

You are a genuine work of pure fake intentions

I know that you will never be a true friend to anyone in life

What goes around comes around

Hope you fucking suffer beyond what words can describe!!!

Tears in your eyes as you lay in filth and emotional decay

WHAT BULL SHIT

Finally thought I met someone

Someone who cared and understood

But when they asked questions

It wasn't what they wanted to hear

Well I am so fucking sorry!!!

Sorry for being fucking honest

I'm not here to play little fucking mind games

Tell you up front what I am looking for

Tell you up front what I want

If you don't agree with me

Then it's fine with me

But don't look at me like I am some...

Some evil fucking creation to ruin your world

You have no fucking idea of what it feels like

The pain that festers inside of me

The pain that twists every nerve into separate rooms

All locked away full of misery, pain & agony

So don't sit there and judge me

Judge me because I am cautious

Because I know what I seek in life

I think I know what I want in a person

Oh no I don't think I am perfect

I am so far from it

You wouldn't believe

But I know inside what I need and desire

This is all I have to offer

You want instant gratification

And I can't give you that

And you're not willing to deal with it

Sorry for you

That I don't trust a living thing

That's fucking life

So deal with it…

And forget about my pathetic being

CAN'T SEEM TO FIND

We've been completely done for awhile

I'm a long lost memory in your mind

Who was I?

You don't remember at all

Even if I walked past you at this moment

I've dealt with my broken sacrifice

The choice I know that needed to be made

Trying to rid my body of this disease called love

It's so wicked and evil

It shows no remorse in what we truly feel and need

It just wants to be fed

Sleepless nights will occur over & over

No one to hold tight

Yet it doesn't want just anyone

It wants the one that you can never have again

The one you are habituated to

No matter how painful it is

The weekend is a day away

And I wonder what to do

Go out & about and see what happens

Or stay home & wallow in the pain

You still haunt my mind

You still appear in my dreams

Why don't you fucking leave me alone

Losing my emotions that I could never find

Because if I could find them

I would strangle them to death

What the fuck is my desire?

Just to be normal again

Not to feel like this

Wait…

To have never met you

Is my true desire

That's more real than wishing

You were still in love with me

DEATH

Til death do us part

Til the day I die

That's what it was suppose to be

My mind, heart & soul all yours

So many things for us to do

So much we can share

Emotionally & physically with each other

The pleasure & pain

I was willing to do anything

Anything to keep this dream alive

Whatever you wanted

I would do it

Whatever you needed

I would get it

Treated you with so much respect

Despite what all you have done and didn't do for me

You could see the love in my eyes

You knew it was real

You knew my emotions were fragile

Handle with care

That's all you had to do

If you didn't want me

Then walk away

My love would have still been there

Hoping the best for you

That wasn't the choice you made

You kept my emotions spinning

Twirling around in my mind

Twisted and knotted in my heart

You pushed it too far

I tried to deal with it

But finally deep inside I finally did die

Then on that Sunday...

I said good-bye

INTESNITY

Once we were something special

Now the bond is no longer there

Like a book that has been read a thousand times

Our spine is now tattered and torn

The pages of our history flying off into the cold wind

You fucking piece of shit

Why do you exist?

Why were you born?

To torment and taunt me?

Laugh in my face

Because all of it was a joke

For your own amusement

There are no secrets

I know all about you

A living thing that tells

Lies upon lies

To acquire all that you need and desire

I didn't ask for this shit!!!

You did!!!

You approached me

You invited me into your life…

Why did I accept that passport to hell

Can't someone revoke it

Stop this idiosyncrasy

The spiraling confusion

Why am I fucking missing you

When I know you are fucking someone else

Most likely at this moment as I write this

Oh yeah you know I am

I am so fucking pathetic

Wishing you were here

Laying next to me…

I'm a fucking idiot

So I guess I deserve it…

As usual it's my entire fault

FULL CIRCLE

Round and round you're back again

Making your presence known once more

Calling and talking to me as if nothings changed

Joking around with a smile on your face

Everything is the same that's how you think

I'm not going to say anything

I won't roll my eyes

Not going to be rude

What's the point

It won't repair the past

What's broke will always be broken

Can it ever be repaired?

Look into my eyes and tell me that it can

I tried to pretend and put a bandage over it

Over & over for a year the wound wouldn't heal

It rotted away seeping with your diseased love

I had the thread for the stitches so I could close it off

But you were the only one with that needle in your hand

The needle that would seal off that emotional hole

You choose not to use it, it never crossed your mind

You just stabbed the needle into both of my eyes

Did you ever think I had emotions inside

Oh wait…

I forgot you only worry about yourself

And every other fucking loser partying all night

With you or around you

Even now when you tell me you missed me

It doesn't come from the bottom of your heart

I know it's a lie programmed in your mind

Etched so deeply in that you believe it's the truth

Sometimes when I look at you

Your so called innocence fools me

You seem so sincere in your deceitful lies

And I know this is one circle…

A circle that will always be broken

With no perfect ending in sight

HOLD ME

You can't stop me now

You've pushed me so far past the edge

We've reached the boiling point

And my blood has turned to shades so bright

That your eyes will burn when you look at me

If you actually really wanted to

But we know deep down inside

What lurks in that cavity you call a chest

Not a beating heart but a cold black stone

That will never shed a drop of anything for anyone

You don't care…

We both know it and the world knows it

To walk away from you is what I want

Let me travel down a path

One that leads anywhere where you are not

Never to see or hear you again

Not to know every curve and angle of your face

To finally never have thought about you

Never long for you on a cold winter night

To never ever have missed you

Never be surprised by anything you do

To never hope that you will call me on the phone

Never be at a show together

Never burn you another CD

Never bring you food in bed

So many of the amazing experiences

Things that I once thought were special

We once shared are now negative thoughts

You had me wrapped around your finger

I was at your slightest whim

Finally now you can't hold onto me…

It's last call

Too late

GOOD F***ING BYE

Bye

Bye

Forever

TURN

We turn everyday

Left or right

Up or down

Wrong or right

It's in our DNA

From the day we are born

We turn and squirm

Towards Mom or Dad

Or whoever is there to love us

Through out our lives we continue

To turn

School we turn

Away or towards

Those that accept

Or those that torment

Later in life

We constantly turn even more

Towards those relationships

Back and Forth

To and Fro

Til finally we assume the

Circle is complete

We are stationary and content

Heavenly bliss

But it's an illusion

Turned away from you for one year

Now you are back

You are my friend

So I won't turn my back on you ever

But I wasn't good enough before

So what makes the difference now???

So I must turn away from anything more

Goodbye…

AT THIS TIME

Too much emotion inside

Swirling around like a black hole

Festering and poisoning me

Slowing me down in life

Feelings too intense

Too much too deal with

Put a hole in my head

Let it all drain out

Wishing it would stop

As soon as possible

Fade away to nothing

Emptying my body as a vessel

A vessel full of anger and pain

Let me dry out feel the heat of a new day

May that heat open my eyes

And sear them blind towards any of your actions

So that I may become immune to you and your cruel ways

So I can stand and walk

Lift my head up high

Leaving me new and clean

Untainted by your disease

Untainted by your ignorance

Untainted by your disgust

To start over again

Move on again

Cherish life again

Be one again

Talk again

Share again

With someone else

But that's not the way

That's not how it was or is

I wish I wasn't addicted to

The one I love

At this time

EARLY MORNING

It's early morning

Somewhere in the six o'clock hour

Just a little bit of light

Shining through the blinds

And so cool outside

Such beautiful weather

Reminds me of Cali

Do you remember when?

On vacation

Das Bunker one night

We were so buzzed and feeling good

Hanging out with friends

Then another club the following night

Meeting new people

From the club we hung out at a friend's place

I was trying to make you be bad

Yeah I guess I am bad in a way

We had such a good time

A time I thought I would always remember

That night & morning was intense

Then back to our room

7:30AM…incredible passion

Maybe some of the best…

Fell asleep then they kicked us out

Too bad there's only a photograph from that night

That I don't even possess

To remind you of what happened

And you'll never see it

Just as you will never see me again

Those are fading memories

Washing away in sin

Draining down into the gutter

The gutter of my dreams

To the black acrid sewer

That was once my heart

TORTURED

Why do I love you

Why do I miss you

Why do I adore you

Why do I want you

Why do I feel that I need you

Why do I think of you all hours of the night

Why do I miss you all day long everyday at work

Why do I see you at the bottom of my drink

At 4:30AM in the Double Down

Why will I do anything

Why will I call you back

Why will I loan you my truck

Why do I take you to the movies

Why do I take you to concerts

Why do I take you on vacations

Why do I feed you

Why do I take you to the doctor

Why do I run to the store for you

Why do I rent videos for you

Why do I give you cards

For no special reason at all

Just because it's you

And you were special

That's all I wanted to let you know

Why did I care so much for you

You meant something to me

But with everything I did emotionally

You never really saw it at all

You take me for granted

Even though…I love you so much

But what good will that do

I'm nothing special

Never was and never will be in your eyes

Just your back-up plan

When you don't find the one..

BETTER

There's always someone better

We know this for a fact

Just like death is unavoidable

The grave beckons our names

Let me pretend we will live forever

Under the black cloud of your illusion

I thought that you were the best

You were the one that changed my views

Opened the silence of darkness

Showed me that I can be at one with the world

Took me to a plateau I never knew existed

I worshipped everything about you

Trusted you with my tattered heart

Let myself fall in love

Or maybe it was just a spell

That you cast upon me with your charming ways

I believed you were someone who was real

Or so I was under the impression that you were

But you knew the same

Along the canyon of darkness

You walked along looking down and observed

As our relationship grew

Knowing there is someone better

And you wanted to find that one

No matter how many you had to go through

While you kept me to the side

Deep in that darkness so far below

To keep you company

When it fancied your mood

Until you find the one you are looking for

Good luck in your journey

Hope you don't feel the pain I felt

Along the way

Because it may wound you for eternity

Like it did to me…

DO YOU???

Remember way back when…

Talk on the phone as soon as we would wake up

Then talk again while we were at work

Agree to meet later

Used to meet during the day

Both of us looking forward to it

That place, you know the little one next to the bar

From work you would drive down

Park and go inside if you arrived first

I would listen to my music along the way

Then when I would get there

I would do the same but actually wait

Wait for you to pull up

Then we can go inside together

The smiles on our faces

Moments forgotten in time

Talk about our day

Order our food

Hold hands, give compliments

Plan what to do that evening or weekend

Share our food & fries, throw away the trash

Leave a tip at the register

Hold the door open for you then walk hand in hand

Hug & kiss you goodbye

Next to your little car then drive back to work

With you on my mind

Can't wait to see you later

Once a week or so we would do this

Something so simple

Yet I appreciated it

Too bad you couldn't

It was all old news to you

That was our lunch date…

Now it's gone forever…

Just like you…

I'm glad

It's best for me this way…

EVERYBODY HAS SOMEBODY

Sick of seeing all these happy couples

Hand in hand they walk all around me

Smiling & laughing, they share something special

Going to the movies

They watch it together

But there's much more behind what they have

Wish I knew the secret

But I can't comprehend

Down by the pier they are everywhere

In a heavenly bliss just enjoying life

And here I am on a never-ending track of having no one

On or Off

It doesn't matter about this train

This train of loneliness is my reward in life

Am I in? Am I out?

What do you think?

I'm the outsider that wants that connection

A connection to someone that is beautiful inside

Someone to guide me if I stray to the wrong

You see them shopping together at the mall

Picking things out for each other

And making suggestions

Makes me so sick

Because I had that once

Reality & gravity slammed me back down

Letting me know I will never be the one

Not for you or anyone else in society

Lost soul with no place to go

Flowing through life no direction

Wondering what will come next

A blind path for me to follow

That leads to never where

The only truth I know is that

Everybody has somebody but I'm sure…

I Fucking don't

And never will…

Ok I guess I am having a bad day

IN TEARS

Why the fuck?

Why am I here?

Why do I exist?

How do you leave this impression on me

That haunts every recess of my mind?

The ghosts linger waiting for a clue

As to why this ever happened

Again and again....

I want to move on

I want to be happy

I want to embrace the life and death

Enjoy it and suffer in pure truth

Not the lies that you portray

Haven't seen or heard from you in months

Unfortunately I am suffering

In tears missing your uncaring self

Flood of thoughts drowning my mind

Refusing to let me swim away

Venus Beach is where I am at

Waiting for the music to rescue me as you swim away

And I am so drowning

None of it matters

Now or Never

I am done

Not done with you, but you've been done with me

Tired of trying for what I can't reach

Why?!?!?! Why?!?!?! Why!?!?!?

Did I have to love you this much

That I was so into you

A waste of my time and emotions

Waste of your time

Some kind of wonderful

The flesh and emotions

But it was all temporary

Til you found someone better....

FIRE

Here comes the clouds

Here comes the rain

A surreal quiet entity waiting to unleash

Those are the days I used to like best

Before this

Over the year there have been none

Now for two weeks

The heavens cry

Tears falling down

Are they sharing my pain?

Do they understand what's inside me?

No one else does & no one else will

Not even you!!!

Is the cool darkness there to put out the fire

The one that you lit deep inside

Deep inside my heart

I'm waiting for it to crumble into ashes

Will the rain wash it away

Wash away the…

New again

Can that actually happen?

I don't know anymore

I wish I wasn't the one to be…

Feel the fire

Let the storm engulf me

Let the lightning strike…

Set me on fire

Make me feel the heat of hell

So I can burn you into nothing

Into a waste of ashes

Nothing important to anyone

As they walk across your remains

Never knowing how much of a liar you were

And then maybe

…I could erase my memories

HALLOWEEN

It's just a couple months away

That was a time we always spent together

Dressing up as freaky as we can

Going to the ball and having fun

This time we won't be together

I'll be with some others

And someone new

I hope you aren't there

But I think you will be

How will I act??

When I run into you....

Will I be fairly over you by then?

And treat you like a friend

I will still show you respect

Even though you never were the one

I still miss you

But I won't let the night be ruined

And let the sadness return

A night out with friends

But I know how you are

And although I'll give you all my respect

I am sure you will do something

Something to hurt me

Just because you know you can

Just because that's how you are

New friends, new people

You just want to prove yourself

Prove that you are the better one

How does that relate to me?

I never did anything to you

So why do you want to hurt me more

Look this hasn't even happened yet

But I feel it inside

Oct 31st weekend

You'll hurt me again

Because you know you can

And you did…

AUGUST 8th

4 more serious conversations

I told you this is it

You don't want to let me go

Yet you still do your shit

You are too busy clubbin'

Hooking up with the bouncers

Hooking up with the bar backs

Hooking up with the bartenders

Hooking up with whomever you can

Hooking up with your co-workers

Hooking up with you best friend's friend

I get a call at 10:00 in the morning

You are suppose to have picked up your kid

4 hours ago

How pathetic are you

You know nothing about the gift of life

Don't try to approach me

I know what the gift of life is

I have seen and experienced both

Life & Death

And appreciate and understand it

My priorities are straight

I know who and what I am

And I adore all of my friends & family

And will be there for them no matter what

So play your games

When you come home

The next night

Sleeping with her ex

I wouldn't really mind

If I knew I was your # 1

But I am not and never could or

Will be

This is the end

Best wishes when time catches up with you

And you are left all alone

FREEDOM CELL

I'm free to do anything but I am still locked down

Locked down by the impression you left

You have scarred me for life

But what can I do?

Nothing at all but try to move on

Move on and away from your hold

Who is at fault

Who will pay the price

I Blame myself for letting you get so far

Letting you entwine your evil tendrils

Into the being that is me

Not letting me get away

Not letting me be whole again

It's still the same nothing has changed

You still party all night and ignore me

You still don't care

Your images and memories float

Float around in my mind

Infecting my only good thoughts

Had to call a friend to make sure

Make sure you weren't informed about a show

I have no problem seeing you

Even though I miss you so

I just don't want to meet your new friends

Especially the one that replaced me

Insecure???

Yes!!!

I use to be your everything

Now I am nothing

Nothing that will ever make a difference to you

I am nothing

I am a nobody in your eyes

As I am here

Locked down inside this Freedom Cell

That will never let me go.........

FUTURE

Time & time again I wonder

Wonder, wonder, wonder

Why do I have feelings like this?

Tears run down my face but why?

Or for what as I squint my eyes?

Missing you like no one else has

Why do I think of you

Why do I desire you?

Why do I need you?

Why are you in my memories

Lurking around messing with my mind

I know there is someone out there

SO MUCH FUCKING BETTER

Someone you can never compare with

That would make you and your presence

Appear like a wisp of smoke

Vanishes away into the night air

Floating away to something new

A place where it can rejoice

Because you always got the best of me

But I have no best

I am nothing to you in your eyes

Nothing good ever does continue to exist

It fades away so painfully

Before I always thought it was you

You, the one who would be there

There 5,10,20 years from now

Of course it was a joke

A joke on me

Just something amusing for you to do

And now I sit here despising

Your entire existence

So I look to the future

Hoping someday

I won't remember you at all…

PICTURES OF YOU

Another fucking day to deal with

Shit is still the same

Nothing has changed

All things invoke memories

This annoying situation

Sunday of all fucking days

Where I want to recover from my adventures

Going through my computer

Coming across 2 years of memories

From the first night hanging out at Tremors

What we considered our first date

Then Cheers afterwards right across the lot

The Melvins and Phunk Junkeez

To the huge concert where you were with your ex

You were in the balcony section and I was on the floor

Comedy shows and movies

How many have we seen

To the Fantasy & Fetish Balls

Dressing up so darkly and both of us pulled on stage with the

IMPOTENT SEASNAKES

And MT's first show at the Cooler

And all of their shows after that

Hooters, The Boston and the final show at The Rock

Meeting Uncle Owen, Cell & Cornerstone

And their friends and friends of friends

Being on national TV at a KILLERS performance at the

Hard Rock

All the times in Cali

From Disney Land to Das Bunker

None of it matters to you…

Does it?!?!?!?

Will it ever…???

I didn't think so…

You are too way above me for that

So why do I bother looking at pictures of you

You would never do the same

DECEIT

Ok Miss "So Fucking Holy"

You say you are so in one with God

God loves you so much

So why do you lie, cheat & steal???

Did God say it's ok to lie your ass off

Did God say you could fuck with their mind

Did God say you could not care about them?

Did God say you were above everyone else?

Did God say you were here to save us all...

Yeah? Save us from what?

Not a damn fucking thing.......

You have not one fucking redeeming quality

Yet in your own mind you are a legend

Loved by all so you can party all night

But in the end you'll pay the price

You have no concept & never will

But do you care?

Hell yeah you don't!!!

Guess what?

No one else does either

As long as they get some from you

They are happy

And you give it up so freely

To everyone that comes your way

Pays for your drink, Gets you inside for free

Takes you out on the town

Buys you food and clothes

Does this make you angry

Well look in the mirror

Without you being so free willed

You could never stand on your own

You are a loser among losers

But that's ok

Just spread your legs

You do it so well

So why did I love you???

SIX FEET UNDER

That's where I want to be

Encased in death

I kiss it's lips

It kisses me back

Total silence

Locked safely away in a exquisite coffin

So deep away from all that tortures me

My eyes shut tight so that I may never see the bad in life

The darkness wrapped around my soul

It's fingers firmly grasping with force that will never let go

Nothing can reach me there

Your thoughts and lies can't touch me

I am finally free of your ties that bind

Bind my soul and heart

From functioning properly in a cold world

Let me make new friends

The maggots, beetles, pill bugs, and earthworms

They accept me for who I am

Not a soul to disturb me

But then again there are others

That are here with me

Tell me their stories

The agony and pain

They have dealt with and have seen

Those that truly mourn them

Making me realize

My life wasn't that bad

I wasn't too far gone

But the damage is done

I wanted to be here

Because of FUCKING YOU!!!

So now I weep over & over again

Not because I want to escape

Not because of your uncaring ass!!!

But because all those around me

Lost so much more than me….

FUCKING FUCKER

Yeah bitch…you know who you are

Look in the mirror

You can't miss that person at all

You're still a low life being no matter what

Born one and will always be one

Draining whoever is near you of their energy and life

Anything you say or do from now on doesn't make a difference

You can't change what you truly are

There is no damage control that you can manipulate

Twist around so that it makes you look good

You've taken what you have needed

Used me for every fucking thing

Used me for my emotions

Used me for my time

Used me for my money

Used me for my honesty

Used me for my sincerity

Used me for all the music I turned

You onto

Hope your having fun with

Your so cool as hell,

Rich friends

Hope they fuck you and

You fuck them like you want to…

Am I bitter?

FUCK YEAH!!!

Am I angry?

Hell Yeah!!!

But that doesn't matter

Once a bitch always a bitch

You can't change the past

You can't change the future

And it will never matter to you

Hope you rot in the gutter

With a slow painful disease

That's all you deserve in life

FARSCAPE

Every episode to 4.5

And the Peacekeeper Wars

Disneyland

San Diego

L.A.

Arc Light

Four Rooms

Memento

Near Dark

Requiem for a Dream

Velvet Revolver

Monsters Inc.

Utopia

Thirteen Ghosts

Fantasy & Fetish Ball

Under World

Dive bars

The Peak Show DVD

Das Bunker

Session 9

Mother Tongue

Brotherhood of the Wolf

Echo Park

A Perfect Circle

Dog Soldiers

Game Boy Advance

Fangoria: Blood Drive

Jeepers Creepers 2

Those wicked brownies

The Eye

Mindless Self Indulgence

28 Days Later

House of 1000 Corpses

My dads death

Fuck you for not remembering

TO THE ONE THAT MATTERS

Why is it that I mean nothing?

Why is it that I'm not worth your time

Not even for a phone call to say hi

That would take 30 seconds of your precious day

Too much trouble for a popular person like yourself

So why do I meet people who appreciate me

Why do they tell me I am special

Why do they actually say someone is lucky to know me

Why do they think I am one of a kind

Why do they think I am unique

Why do they see the good inside me

Why do I walk around with my head hung low

Why am I so lost in my emotions

Why do they know I am not like the rest

Why do I wish or hope to be happy again

Why do I care about other people

Why do people tell me

Tell me I'll find the "one" someday

Just be patient it will happen

Why do they know I am fucking real

Why do people smile when I see them

Why do people appreciate the little things

Why do I respect everyone

Why do I want something concrete in life

It doesn't mean anything to me

Why do I ask why?

Over and over again

Hoping an answer will come my way

It will never come from your lips

The evil of silence rests in you

Because I mean nothing at all to

The one that matters..

You

SIMPLE

What happened when you meet that one

The one that you got along with

You share so many things together

Movies, concerts, shows, pubs

Both of you had decent jobs

Both of you knew what you wanted

You wanted the simple things

Someone to share your life with

Sad or Happy it was shared

You would be there for each other

Guiding and helping each other along

When things went wrong

And you know in this game called life is does happen

You loved each other so deeply

You trusted each other with your hearts

Yet each of you could go off with friends

And do your thing

And again you trusted each other

And no matter what

You knew that's the one you were with

No matter what you fucking did

They still accepted and loved you

For who you were

You didn't have to change to be something special to them

They loved you

They still were willing to do anything

Anything to make you happy and secure

That's what a true relationship is all about

But you didn't appreciate that

You took it for granted

You couldn't see that special thing

You didn't care though

You have better people and things to do

And as usual…

The one that really cares loses out…

FUCKED IN MY MIND

A fucking loser with nothing to offer

Worthless piece of human flesh

A waste to be alive and breathing

And I am not talking about you

You fucking self centered piece of shit

You think it's always about you and only you

Too bad for me that I was and had nothing

What ever I did have to offer

Wouldn't and couldn't meet your standards

I'm just an idiot

Your little trick

A stupid fool

A pawn in your game

A pathetic romantic

A trusting clown

A genuine imbecile

I do have something that I possess now

Where did it come from

How did it arrive in me

The hate boils inside

The temperature rising every minute as I think

On all the ways you made your profitable emotional rewards

On my behalf that I donated to you

Slivers of my heart that can never be returned

You just laugh and laugh...

"Oh poor you. You just want people to feel sorrow for you."

That's what you always say, you heartless punk ass breathing

creation

You fucked me over and over

But it was my fault as well as I bent over and accepted it

Why does this matter

Why does this mean shit? I have no idea

But at this moment in time

11:13PM on a Sunday night

While you are fucking your night away

I despise you to fucking death

ROUTINE

Same shit everyday

The routine is exactly the same

Have a drink and reflect

Have another drink and reflect more

Tears travel down my face

Depression wraps its tendrils around my mind

Squeezing every memory out

So I can suffer as I recall it

It's sweet agony pouring out of my eyes

For what???

We're done and I know it

It's long gone and dead

Buried deep in the black souls of the broken hearted

Never again will life be good

Be good between us

So why do I miss you

Why do I want you

Why do I secretly wish

Secretly wish you call

Miss me you'll say

Yeah right…It's just an illusion

I know you too well

It will never happen

It's just a dream

Not even if you ever lay your eyes

Lay your eyes on my words of emotion

You can read every single page

Of this book

Look at all the pictures I vision in my mind

You'll think about it for a second

Then turn around and walk away

Forget me as you always have

I am nothing…in your mind

As usual

I fade away…

HAPPY....

It's 9:26AM on a Sunday

I'm watching a show on cable

Laughing like crazy all by myself

Looking like a lunatic with too much meds

Feeling this weird sensation

It feels so strange to me

No one to share the joy with

No eyes that I can look into

See that they share the same joy as me

No smile to light up that warmth inside

That existed once upon a time in a place...

No one to wrap my arms around as I roll over in bed

Instead there are tears in my eyes

And what is so awesome

They aren't of sorrow or despair

Tears of joy that I can't explain

Even though I am alone it just feels right

Finally for the first time in ages I am ok

Thinking about L.A.

Wishing I was there

Wishing I was at Bar Sinister

Looking at New York

Wishing I was there

Walking down a busy crowded street

Thinking about S.F.

Wishing I was there

As the fog rolls in covering the cemetery by the Presidio

Looking at New Orleans

Dreaming I was there

Far away from you

Letting it all fade away

So I can start to enjoy life again

Alone or with someone

I finally feel that it can happen

I can be me again

Yeah…in time I will be happy

NO CHANGES

The thoughts of my mind have finally become true

It's exactly as what I have always known

You haven't changed one little bit

You still think the world revolves around you

No one else matters, you are the queen of it all

You are on your throne of dirt and expect me to bow down

Sorry to break it to your thick headed skull

I won't and never will again

You always took me for granted and you don't care

Now you change it around

Try to put the blame on me

Make me look like the evil bad one that ruined it all

You say you want to say something so badly

So why don't you say it

Speak your mind

You have a mouth that fucking works

You truly believe it's true

Oh wait the truth is something new to you

It's your friend that's the liar

The deceitful one

The one that has influenced you

Even more worse

Than what you were

You'll find out sooner or later that I speak the truth

Hope you can handle it

But for now I am just a liar

No matter what you say

It's lies

Barrel after barrel of fiction

Is what comes from your lips

We went out as friends

Now we are no longer

But you don't want to hear it

Should I really care?

No!!!

You'll never change

So why does it matter

OPEN SHUTTERS

My one shutter window is open

After another long day at work

Next to my computer desk

Always looking, wondering

Every damn day

Waiting, hoping

You'll stop by

See your pretty face

That smile that I adore

Not to make up

But at least to say hi

Just to prove things true

That despite all that has passed us by

You still are a true friend

Someone who does care

But you already know that's a total joke

You sit there laughing behind my back

Slapping your thighs and rolling around on your back

And the night stretches

It's a blanket of pure black

I sit there missing you

Wishing you the best

Hoping you are safe

Wanting you

Needing you

Or so I thought

Loving you for all it's worth

The dark starts to float away

Evaporating in the morning

Leaving me staring at the sun

What's so bright about this day?

Nothing!!!

Yet I make it through…

To sit again by the window

Shutters open and me waiting….

Waiting for the one that will never come by…

REMINDED

Threw away more shit

That has a connection to you

All of these things that someway you touched

Tired of my thoughts spinning

Who, when, where

I don't need that

My mind needs to be clear

Focused on my own happiness and life

Not what I once shared with you

I need to wash all of it away

Out of my brain and into the sewer

Where you really, really belong

So let me take an eraser and clean this chalkboard

Wipe it clean of your images

Wiped clean of your lies

Wiped clean of your fake love

So piece by piece into the trash

My mind becomes uncluttered

Healing at a slow pace

The items I throw away

Nothing really important

Even at Buffalo Exchange

Basically worthless to anyone else

But to me at one time they meant something

Now they don't at all

Except

To take me back in time

A place where I don't belong

And should never be

Where we had so much fun

Making me miss those moments

Hoping to relive new ones in the future

But why?

Why do I miss something that was never real?

You never were and never will be

And that's why I don't want to be reminded of you at all...

HATE

Can't find another world

Where you don't exist

Where you will never cross my path

Where I can be whole again

Where I can actually heal from your emotional beatings

The things you've done

The tricks you have created

Lies you have told

Games you have played

Times you have spaced me

The people you used in my place

Phone calls you've made

To others behind my back

On the cell phone I paid for you to use

You don't deserve to know me!!!

Worthless times spent

Why did I bother

Why did I care

Why did I do so much

For someone without emotion

Someone without a conscience

Someone that isn't truly human at all

I can't stand you right now

At this moment

I am beginning to hate you!!!

Hope I hate you for eternity

And maybe even longer than that if it were possible

So that you can never set foot into my life again

Never,Ever…

Let

Me

Rot

In peace

For fucking Ever

MUSIC IS MY SAVIOR

Music

The most beautiful thing in life

That is what gives me strength

That is what fuels my dreams

That is what helps me along

That is what makes me hang on

Music

That is what greets me every morning

That is what kisses my ears to sleep at night

That is what gives me hope

That is what fills most of my day

That is what makes me smile

That is what can change my mood

Music

That is what makes me sad

That is what brings tears to my bloodshot violet eyes

That is what goes with me on trips

That is what is there when I am alone

That is what brings me tears of joy

That is what is there when I am with friends

That is what is there when I go out at night

Music

That is what is real

That is what I share with other people

That is what exists and has a meaning

That is what has a soul

That is what makes this world tolerable

That is what will never leave me

That is what you will never understand

That is what you will never ever know

Music

That is the only thing that will never betray me

It takes a special person to love and understand music

Unlike you

That's all that remains

That's all I have

I'M SO SCARED

12:46 fucking AM on a weeknight

What's going on, what am I doing

Tears like a pathetic bitch

Dripping from my eyes

Where am I going, what am I going to do

Will I grow to be old and alone

Will I never find the one

Will it always be this way

I have so much to offer

But who fucking cares

Not a god damn fucking soul

So I guess this is the way

This is a part of the shitty thing called life

Deal with being fucked over by friends & lovers

Pour out your heart for all the wrong reasons

Then let it be trampled til it's crushed

Crushed into a fine powder

That they can snort

To get high off of your misery

I know there are others out there

Like me

True souls with intense emotion looking for the same

Can you hear my plea

I don't want to die alone…

But it will always be this way

SAD

Going through all my stuff

Came across so many CDs

Pictures of you all over

From the Xtreme Thing Concert

At the Silver Bowl

To the very first…

1-25-2002

The very first date/meeting

You showed up by yourself

At Tremors

Do you remember?

Probably not

Nothing worth your time or thoughts

That was the night everything changed

In so many ways that I never expected

The start of a journey into a hell so painful

Didn't know it would be like that

Didn't know you were heartless

You only cared about yourself

I never lied to you

I never cheated on you

I never abused you

Mentally or physically

I adored all of you

You were always on my mind

All those pictures show us so happy

But maybe it wasn't real

You weren't happy

Happy at one time?

Maybe?

Hopefully?

Guess not

The truth hurts

You aren't next to me now

And there will never be an explanation

SELFISH

You even admitted it…

That you are selfish and don't want

To let me go…..

I'm like your emergency reserve

Until you find the perfect one…..

So I sit here and wait

A patient fool with time on his hand

Hoping and wishing

Wanting what I can never really ever have

Thinking maybe once it will happen

You will open your eyes and see me

Standing there with unconditional love

But that's just a fantasy

You need to do your own searching

Looking and hunting for that one

But that's gonna take time

Weekend after weekend

Drink after drink

Kiss after kiss

Trying to see who it is

Is it this one?

Is it that one?

Or maybe that other one I met a few hours earlier

While I wait in the corner

Rejected and disgusted with your lies

The truth is all that I ask for

Yet you can't do that

Not one decent sparkle in your heart

So I hope & pray you'll stop your games

So whose to blame?

I can't say it's you

I sit back and take this

Creating my own ruin....

I have to end it

Burn the pain so eventually I will be numb to you

IT GETS BORING

Every weekend over & over

Like a perfectly oiled clock

That never needs to be set or adjusted

You reenact & run your little routine

Do your thing to make yourself attractive

Dressing yourself to the nines

Even though it's one of the same outfits out of three that you own

That you wear every time all the time

Walking all confident to your destination

A little buzz in your head

You arrive at your second home

See familiar faces that light up at your sight

You dance and party til

The sun comes up

Swaying to the music

Hook up with whoever

Glances your way and kisses

Your sweet little ass

Let them buy you a drink

You listen to the smooth talk

And go with the flow

It's all BS but you don't care

As long as they supply the drinks

They have your full attention

The intoxication and your friends corrupt you

But repetition is your mode

It is what you are use to and know

Since you have no goals

Nothing that you want to achieve

Nothing to look forward to in life

Months or years later…..

It finally gets boring

And your hand reaches for mine

Searching for that comfortable security

But it's too late…..I'm gone

OTEP

Another weekend come & gone

Same old boring story

You might as well have a commercial

I'll call you back in a little bit

That call never comes

It's your style

I am so use to it

Yet I won't allow it

I don't want it this way

You are too busy with everyone else

Who cares about me....

Not you...

It's never you that cares

So why I am in love with you

I just don't know

I'm grasping at straws that don't exist

Two fucking serious conversations

We tried to make things right

And nothing has changed...

Everything is still exactly as it was before

Chaos of the mind and soul

You saw the CD the other day

Said that you wanted to go

Made a comment then returned to your world

Now it's Sunday and the weekend is done

You call me to do something

Not because you desire to see me

It's because you're bored

Too bad this time

I'm going to see a performance

Hang out with real friends

Witness a real woman

With talent and passion

…and I won't think of you

Not one damn bit…

KEEP YOU BUSY

That's exactly what I am

When you have nothing else to do

The back up plan

The pathetic human being

Who can occupy your precious time

But it's never precious anymore when I am around

I am just a filler

A generic poor substitute

For another being with a better game plan

I quickly vanish from your mind

When whoever calls you for something better

And I keep letting it happen over and over

Every day, Every night

Every fucking week, every fucking month

Every year, every damn time

Hoping one day it might change

Wishing I was important again

Where I'll be number one

And no one else will matter

What fucking diseased bullshit

We both know it will never happen

Not now

Not in the future

My use has come to a halting end

The candle has been extinguished

That use to burn in my heart

Burned for you not so long ago

I'll never be good enough for you

Never look good enough

Never kiss good enough

Never fuck good enough

Never be rich enough

For your sorry ignorant and materialistic ass

The only thing I'll ever be good enough for

Is to keep you busy when you are bored

TO REPLACE

Why do I need this?

Why is it the only thing?

I need someone there…

Someone everyday

Someone to call me for no reason

Call me just to say hi!!!

Someone I think about as soon as I awake

Someone I'm thinking of as I fall asleep

Someone who crosses my mind

More than the natural male's thoughts of sex

Someone who I will truly miss

Even though it's only an hour that has gone bye

Someone who I can trust

Someone who I know cares

Someone who will hug me tightly

Someone who actually wants me to be happy

Someone who wants to share their life

Someone who knows what they want

Someone who won't turn their back on me

Someone who I know will be there

Someone who will make me forget about "you"

Someone to erase you from my mind

It's been a year

And I haven't found them yet

I'm so fucked…..THANKS!!!

THE CONSEQUENCE

Bring it on mother fucker, come on!!!

You wouldn't walk away from this game that you played

You had already won, you got what you wanted

Why didn't you just let me go

Nope to simple for you

Had to drag it out and shove my face in the mud

Let me taste the lies of you

All the dirt hidden behind your wide open eyes

You choose to have it this way

So now deal with it…

You ignorant piece of shit

I am so done

I'm not gonna kiss your sorry ass

Look out for you every minute of the day

Take you places and pay for everything

Oh wait, you have a new little toy

That's rich beyond me

In personality and wealth

So now you are taken care of so well

And now I don't fucking matter

And never will again

Like a loser in a demolition derby

I have been retired forever

Beaten and battered the damage is done

You've inflicted it so well

Didn't feel it til it was way too late

The blade nicking every aspect of my heart

And that's ok

I'm learning to deal with it

Because you'll be there one day as well

What goes around comes around

The consequence is that you'll pay

For your actions

Sooner or later

And no one will be there to catch your fall

I hope you break your spiritual neck...

SOMEHOW MUSIC

The music is flowing everywhere

All around penetrating my ears

I'll never deny it

I always embrace it

It's my first love

And now my only love

It's what helped me make it through

It has kept me hanging on

It pushes me to survive

But you are there!!!

Almost every fucking song…

90% of the time it seems it's all about you

So what do I do?

Bow down and worship your sorry ass

Sculpt a statue for your remembrance

If I did

Should I shatter it now

You're not the one and somehow I know

I know it deep in my heart

What a waste of time it was for me

For me to give you a part of my life

A part that you just tossed away

Did it make a difference to you at all?

We know the answer is no

And it will always be

You'll never change

I was used

Just like the next one, and the next, and the next

You're just a user

Emotionally & physically

If I didn't have feelings

It wouldn't matter

But you are the one who asked me into your life.......

Why did you do that?

Accepted your invitation

My own free ticket to misery and hell

SHOW

Saw you at the show

Had a feeling you would be there

Got a round of drinks

Then I saw you in the distance

Standing there with your friends

Dressed up so crazy

Looking all good as usual

Your eyes scanning the crowd

Not paying attention to what they were saying

I didn't approach you at all

Even though I wanted to

I respected your privacy

Why would you want to see me anyway

Although I wanted

Just to say Hi and get a hug

Give me a link to the past

Remember fond times that no longer exist

Then you noticed me

I know you did

Then you ignored me

Your new friend looked over twice

So I knew it was a lost cause

A few years of our lives we've shared together

And I can't even get a Hello?

I guess I didn't mean anything to you

Or you hate me that much

Hey…maybe it's both

I wouldn't doubt it

You can be totally like that

Good luck with your life

It's time for mine

And now it's time for me once again

To stop missing you

And move on far away from you forever

And ever

TASTE

Twirling like a fool in this thing called life

I'm losing my mind again

It's journey of a well-traveled path

The path of pain and misery

Every thorn scraping my skin

Every rock bruising my body

Every sight pausing my heart

Every turn leading me down

Further into a wicked maze

Towards a complicated mess

So entwined in a vine of lies

My heart rests in its coffin

No longer beating for a soul

Not even mine

No being can understand this pain

Buried alive, was I the sacrifice?

Yeah I sacrificed myself!!!

I thought I had to pay the price

But to exactly who or what?

I never did you any wrong

That's what I wonder

Once I actually thought I knew

Who I could trust

Who was there at my side

Through the ups and downs

But now I know I don't

Every time you resurrect me…

Resurrect me for your own design

I'm whole again for a short time

Then here comes that nervous breakdown

It slams me against the wall of life

Not letting me touch secure ground

Taunting me with its demon smile

It only allows me a taste…

…a taste of what I can never have

THE DAY AFTER

The night was so intoxicating

The darkness was so thrilling

Beyond anything I could dream of…

Imaginations running full tilt wild

Audio ecstasy times a million

Stars lighting my way

The bands were so beautiful…

Playing their music with such intense passion

People everywhere, so much to take in

All there for the same reason

The pulsating beats across, through, and around every cell

Letting the music hypnotically take you

On a audio journey

Places so wonderful to travel to

Haunting pleasure tingling all over my body

What more could I ask for?

What more could I desire?

Something that hasn't happened in a long while

At that time I was sharing the experience

Sharing it with someone I care for

Someone who makes my eyes light up

Someone who treats me like I am special

And meeting all of these wonderful new people

Later at an after party

Hanging out and having so much fun

You can feel the surreal joy in the air

Sensations all over the skin it's pure pleasure

So deep that it touches our souls

My mind wanders a psychedelic road

Floating on pure adrenaline

Drifting higher and higher

Touching the sky and more

And the day after it continues on…

It wasn't you

And never could be…

TO BE KNOWN

How can I be popular?

The way you are

How can I have people love me

Love me for no real reason

Just because I smile at them

And look their way

Have them adore me for nothing else

Not because I am nice

Not because I respect people and their feelings

How can I be like you

People falling all over there feet

Just to kiss your sorry ass

How can I be in a magazine

My picture all over the country

People walking up to me

Walking up to me and saying hi

Hoping I'll engage them into a conversation

Talk to them about nothing at all

Saying hi because they recognize me

Letting me in first

First in line at the clubs and restaurants

Being treated like a VIP

Even though no matter what

I'll never really be that special at all

Special like you

Aren't you so lucky

How can I get free things all the time

Receiving love from all the people like you do

Maybe a thousand would actually appreciate me

More likely a lot less

But there's only one that matters

And that one will never care….

Is life worth it???

TAKEN AWAY

I know you are gone

Someplace somewhere else

We'll never see each other again

Our paths will never cross

No more drinks at the pub

No more shows to see

Hopefully it will stay that way

The connection has been severed

That thing we had no longer exists

And I know it was my choice

It was something that had to be done

Try to move on with my life

Let me breathe all that is good

Instead of the poisoned smoke

That you emit from your pure black heart

You said you would miss me

Yet you haven't called once

You've not even tried to stop by

You've never drove by to see if I am here

Even though you are near

At least a few times a week

You still have some of my belongings

You probably have thrown them away

But I guess the new one

Is that good

Floods your mind with their essence

You already hardly think of me

Now it's 100%

The fate of death has been sealed

My memory is on its deathbed

And now I no longer exist

I guess all of the memories

From the last few years

Were never real things in this dimension

So why are you still on my mind?

THE 13th

I'm so tempted to call you

Just to say that I got you something

Some incredible clothes that you might like

I know you would look so good in

Even though we aren't together

Still I want you to look beautiful

Why ???

What the fuck is wrong with me???

Why should I make you look good

Look good for someone else…

So they can enjoy the view

All the benefits plus more

I'm just a fuck up!!!

I'm just an idiot…

The same idiot that you met that 1st night

The one that fell for your wicked ways

And I'm still that one

Blinded by love

Trying to find the way back into a paradise

That has long since been destroyed

Searching for a way into an empty place

Where nothing of value can ever exist

Here, take my money

Here, take my credit cards

Here, take my truck

I'll never be happy again

So why do I need any of that

So why do I feel that I need you

So that I can feel complete again?

Yeah the jokes on me

Good luck in your life

I'm sure you are happy!!!

So fucking happy

You're so shallow

Remember what goes around comes around

Double the amount my former friend, that's just the way of life.

SKINDRED

Yeah, you remember them

I turned you onto them over

Two years ago

The stupid corporate ass station is now

Finally playing them

Just heard on the radio

They're playing here Sept 9th

Goosebumps crawled all over my body

I wanted to call you

Tell you I got tickets

Then the sadness ripped it's way in

Letting me know this is a lost cause

All of those shows we went to together

So much music we shared together

So many bands I introduced to you

So many CDs that I gave you

So much emotion when I hear things

Things that we use to listen to

What happened

What went wrong

We had a love

It's all over

So many fucking memories

Way too many shows

Too many people that knew us as a couple

Tears run down my eyes because

It's all gone forever

Those times are long gone

Faded away into the past

Never to be reunited with you or me

Kiss it good bye

I did regretfully

This show we won't share

I'll be there alone

I just hope I won't see you there

SEE

I don't mind what I can't see

I can deal with what is hidden

I can cope with it all

You already know that

Yet you pushed the limits

Just to see where you could go

Because in reality you didn't care

Step away and let me breathe

Stop playing your immature games

Stop fucking with my mind

Play your parlor tricks on someone else

Do you know how old you are?

Oh??

I forgot you missed out on life when you were…

…Were a fucking loser addict

Well you were happy & high then

Having a fucking good time

So exactly what did you miss out on in life?

Now you have to make it up at my emotional cost

Well you shouldn't have invited me into your life

I told you where I stood

Now I am dealing with these emotions

Because of you

And you still don't understand how I feel

And you never will

You never gave a fuck

So why do I deal with this BS?

Why did it go this far?

Why did you play your games

Assuming all was good

I'm just an idiot

I guess I saw something in you that was real….

But now I know it was a lie

Just like every inch of your living being…

STANDING TO THE SIDE

I'm invisible like a meaningless fly on the wall

Yet I am standing there plain as the cold winter day

With miles of pure white snow

Standing in black & purple

Hard to miss

I brought you here

And not one bit of your conscience cares anything at all

Rubbing up on that bouncer and getting a kiss

Who am I?

Just a fool who isn't a priority

We haven't talked in two months or more

Then all of a sudden we're friends again but I should have known

the deal

Getting along so well and I wasn't hoping for false expectations

Yet you play it off like it was all beautiful

Covered everything

Not one thanks

What the fuck am I to you?

Some stupid fool you keep on a long leash

I never asked to be something in your life

You're the one who approached me

You're the one who asked

You're the one who thought I might be something good

But in the end I see the true you

I never could be good enough no matter what

For me to respect, honor and adore you

Something you can't grasp

So thanks once again for lowering my self esteem

Telling me I am special then stepping away

Into your own private VIP crowd

Do you remember back when I did all I can

Anything and everything for you, what was I doing?

DAMN!!!

I know no one exists that is totally perfect

Yet I adored all of you and thought you would never deceive

But you could and you did it well or so you thought

Voice mails, business cards, seeing you kissing with my own two

eyes

Etched in my mind

Being in love makes you lose your view

I see it, I feel it, I know it, I hide it

And yet you don't know what

Lost as usual

All this agony and pain that I keep inside

When we see eye to eye you have no idea

I'm just happy so I keep it within

Why should I let you know?

You already destroyed my heart

Memories fade away they always do

But why won't this, why won't you?

Just vanish from every single cell in my mind

So I don't have to hide from the truth

The truth is 100% real and genuine unlike what's in your soul

In the course of a year your inconsiderate manners

Have ravaged my heart

Like the waves crashing against a beach so serene

You keep slapping me in the face

Burying my self worth down deep so it can never be viewed

Time, time, time and time again

I expose and express myself

Because you say you want to know what's on my mind

But nothing changes and the tide continues with its treacherous

flow

You float along calmly without the slightest care

While inches away I am drowning gasping for the love

That never existed

So into the cold depths I sink to the bottom

Into the black darkness for my soul to keep

All the misery and pain, I remember all of the things I let slide

Good things come to those who wait

Guess what?

Time was never on my side

I ask myself is there anything possible that I can actually change?

You're in a circle of friends and a lifestyle that is out of my reach

I'll never qualify to be that important in your eyes

I'm just worthless trash with the flies and maggots

Rotting, decaying, slowly wasting away

The beating of my heart no longer has something to speak

It's dead and silent a petrified wall of pathetic despair

With no desire or destination

Will anyone show me the way out

Once upon a time I was sitting on the edge of something

So beautiful & grand

But you pushed me off with your selfish ways

Side by side a perfect couple or so I thought

The charade is over and now I know

Caught in your web of lies so sticky and thick

One time on the phone with you I felt something like an

epiphany

No matter how hard we try we'll never touch the stars and moon

And in the end

Time does not heal all wounds....